A VERY YOUNG PSYCHOLOGIST IS BORN

A VERY YOUNG PSYCHOLOGIST IS BORN

D.B CLARK

EDITED BY CAROL CLARK

A VERY YOUNG PSYCHOLOGIST IS BORN

iUniverse books may be ordered through booksellers or by contacting:

iUniverse
1663 Liberty Drive
Bloomington, IN 47403
www.iuniverse.com
844-349-9409

ISBN: 978-1-6632-0302-1 (sc)
ISBN: 978-1-6632-0303-8 (e)

Print information available on the last page.

iUniverse rev. date: 08/26/2020

CONTENTS

INTRODUCTION

This is a fantasy, based upon a clinical psychologist should perform, but actually performed by the protagonists, Daniel (nickname Danny) James. As he becomes a premature psychologist, and while playing with his friends, teaches them, as is a psychologist's job, to manage their own problems, probables usually caused by their parents. Therefore, as is so often the case, the child teaches the adult.

William James (January 11, 1842 – August 26, 1910) was an American philosopher and psychologist, and the first educator to offer a psychology course in the United States. James is considered to be a leading thinker of the late nineteenth century, one of the most influential philosophers of the United States, and the "Father of American psychology".

Along with Charles Sanders Peirce, James established the philosophical school known as pragmatism, and is also cited as one of the founders of functional psychology. A Review of General Psychology analysis, published in 2002, ranked James as the 14th most eminent psychologist of the 20th century. A survey published in American Psychologist in 1991 ranked James's reputation in second place,[10] after Wilhelm Wundt, who is widely regarded as the founder of experimental psychology. James also developed the philosophical perspective known as radical empiricism.

My First Questions

What does an infant know after he is born
That he didn't know before.
Even before he was born,
He must have known his Mother loved him.
He must have known, or at least felt,
That his Mother believed him to be
A being of god-like form.

But Infant Danial (Danny) Williams
Not only knew or felt his Mother's love,
He wanted to know why.
Moreover, he wanted to know the whys of lots of things,
Like why do people, even his mother, have to die.

This is the story of an obviously precocious child
Who asks himself the profound,
And sometimes disturbing questions,
*That **adult** psychologists ask.*

Now this actual psychologists, D. B. Clark,
Is asking you to ask yourself these same questions.
And if you are able to answer them,
Maybe you are as smart as Danny Williams.
But, honestly, I think, in reading this book,
You will find that no one is as smart as him.
But, who knows? There are some knowable parents,
And maybe you are one of them.

Here is some of my family history that I became aware of as I grew past infancy. We lived in Birmingham Alabama. My father was a bricklayer who, with his crew of sometimes five black men, layed the brick work on houses and small business buildings. We were lower middle-class, and my friends were generally of the same class level.

Both my parents finished high school, and my mother was a clerk in a small bossiness. I attended a good public school, and soon came to believe that I was maybe smarter than my friends. But that wasn't important. They were my friends, and as far I a was concerned, we were all equal.

Until my friends started having problems That's when I realized that my friends didn't consider me just like them. The questions they stated asking me said they knew I was smart, maybe super smart. And when I started answering their questions, and they looked so relieved and grateful, I began to get big headed, particularly when one of my friends said my answers sounded like what he had heard when he and his parents had gone for parent-child counseling.

Then, whoa! That sounded like a prideful brat that I knew, and if I was to be my friend's psychologist, I should have better control over my pride.

So, then I began to learn something else about being a psychologist, even though I was to be only a boy psychologist. In helping my friends, I had keep in mind that I also had problems, and if I didn't effectively manage my own problems, I might pass those problems onto my friends.

NICOTINE ADDICTION

Don't Force, and Heal

Don't try to force the body to heal,
Allow it to heal:
Don't take drugs,
Don't over-stretch,
Don't run long hours.
Instead, meditate, meaning, don't move.
And then take deep breaths,
And then small breaths,
And then no breaths at all.
And after that, if you're extremely patient,
Renewed Health will call.

So, don't try to force the body to heal.
Allow it to heal,
And then have confidence that you will appreciate
What you feel.

This is my first, and very important case. When I was six years old, I asked Father why he smoked cigarettes. He said, I would know when I was older. But I wanted to know now. So, I went to my room, rolled up piece of paper, lit up the end, *and sucked in fire!*

That's stupid! I told myself, and I wanted my father to be too smart to do such a stupid thing. So, I guess this means my Father was going to be the first I helped.

I went back to my Father and told him what I had done. And I told him that I thought I was stupid. (I have the right to judge myself.) And I said that I wanted him to stop burning his lungs.

My father started to object, like no six year old boy was going to tell him what to do! But then he paused, and looked sheepish. "Son," he said, "I know smoking isn't good for me, and I've tried stopping, but somehow, I always end up starting again." Then he actually seemed depressed.

Then I grew eager to help. "Daddy," I said, you're my world's best Father. We can lick this problem together!"

I was pleased that my Father began to seem hopeful. "Well what do we do, son?"

My young psychologist brain kicked into gear. "Here's my plan. Tell me what you think about it. Give all your cigarettes, I mean all of them. I'm going to place them some place very inaccessible down in the basement. You will have climb up on the latter to reach them.

Then, to stop you from going to all that trouble, tell me what is happening. What I will do then, is ask you lie down, and I will teach you how to breathe very, very deeply. Let's try it right now. Lie down on the couch, and start breathing. Deeper! Deeper!

"Good. That's it. That's it. Now relax, relax!"

Sure enough, my Father looked relaxed.

I nudged him. "How about it, Daddy, do you want a smoke?

My father looked startled. "Damn it! I mean darn it, I could care **less** about having a smoke! How did you know how to do that, son?"

I was puzzled myself. "I don't know, Daddy. It just popped into my head."

My Father smiled. "I always knew you had a brainy head. Must come from your Mother."

Then, he became concerned. "But my workers will be offering me cigarettes, and I'll probably be weak."

"You might want to think of yourself as week, but Super Father isn't weak. So, here's what you do. Tell your workers that your young psychologist son is curing you of your cigarette addition, and he wants you to smoke away from me. They like and respect you, so they will probably laugh about yout six year old boy being your psychologist, but thry will do what you ask."

My Father grabbed me and hugged, laughing, "Is it okay to hug your psychologist?'

I don't know about okay, but it sure felt good.

BODY IMAGE CONCERNS

At least I Remember When

I fell in love with you in the Spring,
And my Summer love was rapturous
And I was sure this love would always be a part of us.

But now it's December,
And it's difficult to remember
How I had fallen in love in the Spring.

But do not worry, my Dear,
Winter will soon be over,
And Spring will again do its thing.

And I will fall in love again,
For that is what happens to men
When they grow older,
They fall in love again,
But only now and then.

I had often seen my Mother staring at her body in the mirror, turning this way and that, and looking unhappy. Then she would shake her head, look away to put on her office clothes.

Finally, I decided to ask her, "Mommy, why do you always look so sad when you look at your image. I think you are beautiful."

"That's because you're my loving son, and anyone who has such a loving son has to have beautiful mother."

That didn't sound logical to me, but I let it pass. "Anyway, Mommy, you're the one who seems to think you're not beautiful, so as your loving son, I just want to make you happy, because you're already beautiful."

"It seems my loving son is also a diplomat, but clever as you are, you can't fix the unfix-able, I was just born to be fat."

"Like skinny Granny was fat?"

"Okay, you got me there, smarty pants, but enough discouraging talk, I have shopping to do before I go to work."

But I must have shown how concerned I was, so she stopped to listen

"Mommy, since you know I love you, my must know I have to make you unhappy. So, will you let me try?"

That brought her up short, "Well, since you're so insistent, okay."

"Good, good! Here's what I'm going to do. You know it's all those sugar goodies that that make maybe a little overweight."

"The diplomat again, you mean fat!"

"I mean overweight. I'm going to sit in the shopping cart, and every time you put a sugar goody in the cat, I'm going drop it on the floor, and if it's in a glass jar, it's going to make a mess."

My Mother looked a little chagrined at that.

"And then, if you don't head directly toward a real food isle, I'll pick up another glass jar."

That motivated her to head where I told her, and when we got to the cashier, the cashier remarked, "This is the healthiest shopping cart I've seen all day!"

My mother finally looked happy. "It's my son's doings."

The clerk looked at me, and with a smile, commented, "I see what you mean!"

I started to feel pride, but then reminded myself. The effective psychologist, knows his actual worth, and is not inflated by flattery.

When Mother was dropping me and the groceries at our house, she was concerned again. "But Danny, you know, at the office, all the girls will be offering me their goodies, especially those skinny girls who want to keep fat, so they can feel superior to me."

The junior psychologist was getting more confident. "So, here's what you're going to do. You'll say to those girls, "No, dears, you keep your sugar goodies. You're so slim, you cat eat all those goodies and not get fat. I really do admire you."

"That should stop their tormenting you. It's no fun making fun of a someone who admires you." At that, my Mother only stared a moment, and then broke out into a broad loving smile, before finishing with, "I can do it, son, I can do it!"

And she did. And as the weight poured off, I decided It was okay to feel pride. If a psychologist does effective work, he should reward himself. That probably make him work harder.

ALCOHOL ADDICTION

Awareness is all good

You can be aware of pleasures*,
Which could be either good or not.
The good ones could be good for you,
And the bad ones might hurt you a lot.

You can be aware of happiness*,
Which could be either good or not,
The good ones could be good for you,
And they might just hit the spot.

So, if you want to remain healthy,
Be sure to choose wisely,
Or too much of your happiness and pleasure,
As well as your health will ceace to be.

*Pleasure and happiness are not just feelings, they are represented by neurons firing in your brain. When you feel pleasure, dopamine is being secreted to activate the feeling. When you are feeling happiness, serotonin is being secreted to activate happiness. As indicated in the poem, too much of any feeling might not be good for you. These are some of the good pleasures: healthy foods, a warm bath, being caressed by a loved one. These are some of the bad ones: tobacco, cocaine, sugar, hate. These are some of the good feelings of happiness: loving someone, listening to gentle music, experiencing the sunset. These are some of the bad feelings: superiority, judgments, and revenge.

My Aunt Opel lived across the street from my house, and often, I went over to play with my cousin, Barbie. She was a little older than I, but she had heard about my helping my parents, so I wasn't surprised that she asked for my help.

"What's wrong?" I asked.

"My mother comes home from her piano playing job at the downtown bar all funny."

"Funny?"

"Like, at first she's angry, then she's apologetic, and then she's sad, but always she's wobbling around."

"Like drunk?" I said it for her.

"Yeah, drunk!"

"I understand," I reassured her.

"I guess she gets home this Sunday morning early, so I'll get here at that time to meet with you two, all right?"

So, that's what happened. I sneaked out of my house, and when over to meet Barbie, and see Aunt Opel behaving just like Barbie had said. She greeted me angrily, then looked apologetic, then dismissive, "What are you doing here, Danny?"

"Just came to play with Barbie," I said, then asked politely, "How are you feeling?"

My politeness changed her behavior. She became sad, "Not so hot, honey. Those jerks at the bar keep complaining that I miss the beat on some of my songs, and they laugh and say things like, you're not the concert pianist you used to be."

Then Barbie slipped in, "And you didn't used to drink so much either, Mommy."

Aunt Opel started to get angry again, but then became even sadder, "That's right, it's just that it's so hard playing well when I feel so bad. I just haven't been myself since your father left us.

"But that's been two years, Mommy!

I felt it was time for the Junior Psychologist to take charge. "Aunt Opel, if you really want to be yourself again, are you ready to let me help you?"

A small smile broke out on Aunt Opel's face.

"My sister tells me you are some kind of super helper, so why not."

I followed up on that with, "And your younger sister always tells me that her older sister always knew how to do right. So if you want to do right again, Opel, will you do what I say?"

She paused only briefly before answering firmly, "Yes, Super Danny, yes!"

"Here's my suggested plan. Tell me if you agree to carry it out. When you go back to the bar tonight, put a sign on your piano saying, *The glasses on my piano will contain only silver dollars, no booze!*"

Then take a deep breath, pause and the strike a loud chord on the keys, and then bang out a brief playing a Beethoven sonata."

Then Opeln barked out, "I can do it! I can do it!"

And Barbie echoed that, "You can, Mommy, you can!'

"And then finalize the performance with an arousing set of happy bar-time tunes, bowing to the house applause, after each song."

With that, Opel began pounding an imaginary set of keys, sing a loud song, and bowing to her laughing daughter, Barbie.

Then the both turned to me, and Aunt Opel said, "What your mother said is true, you are super!

I took my own small bow, and then became serious, "But Aunt Opel, you can't do this alone. *Join Alcoholics Anonymous today, before you go to work! Okay?*"

And one more thing. One slip up doesn't make a fatal accident. One drink only means, one drink! Starting getting to get clean the second or third time will be easier."

"And next time, take two aspirin, and call me in the morning."

YOUNG PSYCHOLOGIST, KNOW THY SELF!

A Wise Man once said, Learn to Forgive

Sometimes I get angry when someone does something terrible,
And I can't do anything about it, So I just stop thinking.
Of course, suppressing my feeling is not good for me,
So, eventually I force myself to be my non-suppressing me.

But then I have to accept that I am angry,
And that might also be not good for me,
Especially if I attack that other person,
And he is even angrier I than could ever hope to be.

So, perhaps I should become Buddha-like
And rise above these Earthly feelings,
And meditate on eternity.

But, I am not Buddha, so I guess I will wait until I reincarnate
And hope that in my next life,
I will be able to become a more forgiving me.

As a young psychologist, I had been coasting along, growing ever more confident in my ability to help others, when several experiences taught me that I didn't yet know myself to always effectively help other. Time to stop coasting and start walking up hill.

There was a boy in my fourth grade class who larger than I was, not as good looking as I was, but more mature. When I saw him talking to a girl who interested me, I felt this new feeling . . . envy?

So, I managed to bump into him hard enough that he bumped back, and we started to fight. But because of his size, and the length of his arms, he was punching me harder and more often.

I didn't like what was happening, but I didn't know what to do.

Then someone in the gathering crowd barked out, "You're faster than he is, Danny, circle around behind him, yank him down backwards, and start pounding his face."

I did just that, but before I could start poundin, the school janitor yanked me up and marched us back to the principal's office. I was glad he did. I had never beaten any one, and I didn't think I would like it.

We sat in the principal's outer office glaring at each other, when a small smile slid out on the side of his mouth. And by the time the principal came out to discipline us, we were both laughing.

The principal laughed too, and dismissed us.

From that time, although we were not friends, we were not enemies. But he was still better at getting the girl's attention. And I still felt a little envy. Thank goodness, I was a lot smarter, so at lease the teacher liked me better.

In my next self-discovery experience, I was less successful. One of my best buddies at this age was Shorty, who lived down the block from my house. We played side-lot foot ball, and I was always better, and I was always better at board games, so I guess that's why he had to be better at something he knew I wouldn't do—stealing!

So, one day, he road the streetcar downtown to a department store, and shop lifted two very real looking toy pistols.

He was very proud when he showed them to me. But he was anything but proud when he saw my shocked and, although I couldn't help, judgmental expression.

So, he took my pistol back to the department store, showed it to the shopkeeper, and said he had found in outside the store on the street.

But, he didn't mention keeping his own stolen pistol.

So, what did I learn about my young psychologist skills? Although I didn't believe Shorty was doomed to be a hardened criminal, I didn't yet know how to help my boyhood buddy be only a minor criminal, who might occasionally cheat or underpay on his bills.

And, unlike so many such criminals, he wasn't religious, so he probably wasn't worried that God was going to send him to Hell.

So, what did I learn? Don't be a perfectionist. Being reasonably good is good enough. But as we continued growing up together, I would be there to stare at my friend, Shorty, when he looked like he was about to behave criminally, and hopefully, keep him out of jail.

BIGOTRY

A Certain Identity

I've got it so good, I've got it so bad.
Nobody's got all the good things I've had.
And nobody's life has ever been so glad,
And nobody's life has ever been so sad.

And if you sent me down into Hell,
The Devil wouldn't have me.
And if I were falling out of Heaven above,
God Almighty wouldn't grab me.

So, I guess my the problem is,
I don't really know who I am.
And believe me, I've been trying to know,
But to someone watching, it might seem I really don't give a damn.

So, am I' black or am I white?
It turns out, what I am is somewhat brown.
In other words, it's okay to be whatever I am.
I'm just as good or bad as any other man in
town.

Seek shelter, mournful brethren,
So the enemy cannot find you,
Until your strength you'll regain.
Then, as lightning follows thunder,
You will flash forth again.

But, enemy, even if you turn to stand and fight,
We will always stand above you,
And you will succumb to our might.
And the wrong you have done us will fade,
As wrong becomes right.

I've got it so good, I've got it so bad.
Nobody's got all the good things I've had.
And nobody's life has ever been so glad,
And nobody's life has ever been so sad.

And if you sent me down to into Hell,
The Devil wouldn't have me.
And if I were falling out of Heaven above,
God Almighty wouldn't grab me.

So, I guess my the problem is,
I don't really know who I am.
And believe me, I've been trying to know,
But to someone watching, it might seem
I really don't give a damn.

So, am I'm I black or am I white?
It turns out, what I am is somewhat brown.
In other words, it's okay to be whatever I am.
I'm just as good or bad as any other man is town.

I was not cursed by the Southerner's prejudice against blacks. My Father hired black worker, my working mother depended on Ante Jessie Washington, my nanny and our housekeeper. And on holidays, we had barbecues at black's church parks with black families.

So, I was puzzled by the signs on drinking fountains that said, "Whites Only!"

I asked my Mother about it, and she said that many whites believed that blacks were dirty. I knew that was nonsense. Auntie Jessie's son, Jamie, who was two years older than me, and who oftrn came with his mother to play with me, was much cleaner than I was.

And when I told Ante Jessie this, she laughed, "Child, you couldn't help being dirty. You're always driving your toy cars over small dirt roads in the backyard. and with the coal burning steel mills outside Birmingham, the dirt is coal dust."

That was true, and Jamie wasn't dirty because I had him reading all the library books I had finished reading, before I took them back to the library.

So, dusting myself off, it was time for the Young Psychologist to take charge. "Auntie Jessie, you know I help people solve problems, will you let me help you solve your problem?"

She became as serious as I was. "Sweet Jesus, child, my problem is too big even for someone as amazing as your Mommy thinks you!"

"Auntie Jessie, any problem is too big if you don't try to solve it.," I said quietly.

That caught her attention. "My word, that does sound like you might know something worth listening to."

"Good, here's my plan. I'm going to keep making Jamie read everything I give him, so when he gets to high school, he'll be an honor student, and even so good, he will get scholarships to a black college. You and I will stay after him until graduates and become a lawyer, and famous enough to lead the fight to advance black rights, even in the South. How's that for good plan, Auntie?"

"The Good Lord couldn't have made a better one!" Let's go tell your black brother, Jamie!"

It was a good plan, and I was eager to become an even more effective Young Psychologist against whatever problems I came up against in New Orleans, where the family and I were heading next week.

DEPRESSION

Depression, go Away!

Life doesn't always go as planned.
So, you must buckle down and try again.
And even then, life is sometimes a battle
In which you won't always win.

Buy don't get depressed, get challenged!
Look for and find anther way,
To win the battle. And then you will find
You are able to find you are able
To live life fully everyday.

My father, my mother, and I went from Birmingham, southwestward, across the Mississippi to reach New Orleans. This was mostly rural country, and the home of those black folk some white Southerners considered dirty and inferior. The people I saw were certain were neither dirty nor inferior. Their old clothes were clean, and their faces looked as intelligent as most of those white people's I knew.

We rented a two bedroom cheap apartment in walking distance from my Catholic grammar school. Catholic, because the New Orleans public school were considered inferior.

I enjoyed walk to school, I always left home early, so I would have time to study the neighborhoods along the way. There were the big homes on the front street, and the small servant homes on the every other back-ally. I particularly liked the street that ran beside the vast New Orleans cemetery. On the street side, the wall often had broken open chambers filled with bones. I sometimes poked inside, feeling the bones, and imagining the bones filling out with flesh. But, this didn't scare me. I figured I would talk them, asking what it would be like to be dead. Was there a Heaven or a Hell and all that? Or just nothing at all? I believed that I needed to know the answer to such questions to help my people who were afraid or about to die. I guess I was getting to be a very serious Junior Psychologist.

I learned I was right, when, in walking along the walkway inside the cemetery, I saw ahead of me a man kneeling and bent over a gravestone. I approached quietly, knelt down beside him, and put my hand on his shoulder and asked, "May I help you, sir?"

I guess he was expecting an older person, for when he looked up, he was surprised. "No, son, thanks for asking, but I'm afraid that even a beautiful child like you won't be able to fill the emptiness I feel at the loss of my beloved wife." Then he began crying, "Why darling, why did you have to leave me?"

I realized instantly, that this was going to be a difficult case for this death-inexperience familiar Junior Psychologist, but I knew I had to try to help.

"Sir, perhaps in my childlike innocences, I will say things that will help. May I try?"

The man then wiped away enough of his tears to look at me more closely. He even managed a small smile. "Well, after all, Christ was once a child, and he certainly helped people."

I didn't like being compared to Christ, but I would take the chance someone seemed to be giving me. "Sir. Tell me about your wife, and in particular, I want to hear about how much she cared for you, and how much she would want you to take care of yourself, so you could take care of the others in your family. And, sir, my name is Daniel."

"Yes, yes, I should be polite to someone who is so graciously trying to help me. My name is Jacques Bruussard, and yes, you're right, my wife, Adelaide, always insisted that I should take better care of myself, saying I worked so hard as a mule and had less brains."

"Good, sir, and we are now going to listen to your loving wife. Here's the plan I suggest. Right now, you are going to get up from your long cramped position, and starting walking beside me. And as you walk, you are going to start taking deeper and deeper breathes until you are positively panting. That's it! That's it!"

Now stop, but continue breathing . . . Now relax all over. That's it, that's it. Now tell me how you feel."

Jacques did as I asked, and then slowly began to describe how he felt. "I feel so relaxed, no tension in my belly or chest.

"Would you say you feel good, not bad, and not *even sad?*"

"My lord, you're right. I feel great." Then he laughed, "does this mean I am cured of my . . . depression?"

I laughed also, "No, as your Junior Psychologist, I am not that good. There is more you need to do. Go to those family members your wife was concerned about, and tell them what you just learn about yourself, and ask them how you can help them deal with their depression."

"I'll do it! I'll do it!"

Then stop by your wife's grave every morning at the same time, and assure your wife that you are taking care of yourself and your family."

"And for awhile, I will also be here to ask how you're doing, and you'd better be doing okay, or I'll start charging you more than just a thank you for my very useful services"

His laugh told me that he had made a good start toward managing his depression. But compared to my next case, this case had been easy. My Next case was going to be curing the sins of the Catholic religion!

RELIGIOUS PERVERSION

You be the one who tells you what to do

According to the Hebrew Bible,
We were all born to sin.
So we must spend eternity
Trying to be as good as we should have been.

But whether or not you're a believer,
Since you're human, you'll make a mistake or two.
That doesn't mean that you're going to Hell
When your mistake filled life is through.

I was eight years old, and in the Second Grade in my Catholic school when this happed to me. My homeroom teacher was Sister Virginica, a tall stern teacher who seldomed smiled. As was usual, the girls were on the far left side of the classroom, and the boys were on the far right side of the classroom.

Sister Virginica was lecturing on boy, masterbation. In a threatening tone, she insisted that if we boys did anything more than just hold our penises while urinating, we could be in danger of sinning, we would be condemned to Purgatory to have our hands burned until we burned off that sin. But if we ever actually played with our penises, we would be condemned to Hell to burn forever! Most the boys were giggling, a few looked frignted, but I was outragged!

Therefore, after school was over, I marched into Sister Virginica's office, demanding, "Sister, I believe what you told us boys is not actually Catholic doctorine. So in saying what you said, you would be commiting a sin! And therefore, Sister Virginica, you have sinned, and iyou should burn in Hell!"

Sister Virginica turned red, and spiuttered when she tried to speak. Finally, she blurted out, "Young man, how dare you speak to me like that . . . I'll . . . I'll . . ."

Then I continued on, even more forcefully, "Yes, Sister, I am addressing you as a young man, and not as just a boy. And I'm sure you know from my school record and test scores, I am no doubt the most intelligent student you have ever encountered. And you might have also heard from you school Principle, Father Paul, that I do my best to help people, and most often adults, to fine ways to better manage their problems, or in your case, sins. Then I softened my voice, "So would you like my help, Sister Virginica?"

The Sister's complextion slowly changed from red to almost gray, and when she finally spoke, her voice quavered. "Young man, I mean Daniel, I don't really know what to say . . ."

"How about yes, and thank you for offering. But, Daniel, how can you help me? How can anyone help me? I have been trained to think about sex this way, and you proably have guessed I know almost nothing about sexual behavior," Then she managed a small laugh. And that's probably why Mother Rebecka named me Virginica."

"Good," I said even softer, "I like it that you're laughing at yourself, After all, laughter is said to me the best medicine, so maybe I can help you laugh away your sin. But enought laughter, It's time to get serious. He're the plan I suggest to have you solve your own problem. Hear me out, and if you like it, make it your plan, because in my working with people, I make it clear that they must do all the work. I just listen to and apraise their progress. But right now, let's try a little experiment. I noticed when I first approached you with my accusations, you tured red. Then you turned gray, and at the same time, you clutched your chest and began a slight panting. Were you hurting?"

"Yes, and I'm still hurting a little bit. What can I do about it?"

"The right question, and here's the simple answer *Breethe! dear Sister, breethe!*"

And she did, and very quickly she began to obviously relax.

"And I feel good now."

I laughed, "Good as in nolonger sinning and going to Hell, with all those bad boys like me?

Now the Sister began giggling, like a young girl and no longer the big *Sister Virginica.* "*So* does that mean I'm cured, Doctor Daniel?"

"Hardly, young Sister Virginica. You're not only innocent about sexual behavior, you are also obviously very ignornate. Go to the Publick Library, not the limited school library, and read all the books about sexual behavor, and not just about sexual reproduction, but about sexual pleasure."

Then the Sister Virginica turned red again, so I guess there was hope for her afterall.

PHOBIAS

Phobias are no Fun

All phobias are basically the same,
They are triggered by panic that has been learned.
And obtaining a victory over phobias like
Hydrophobia, claustrophobia,
Agoraphobia, and even triscadicaphobia
Isn't easy. It's a victory that has to be earned.

And you don't unlearn a phobia once it's been learned.
You have to learn a new skill,
And learning a new skill takes time and strong will.
But once that new skill is learned, The
phobia victim will be phobia free.

It didn't take long for us to get back to Birmingham. Auntie Jessica was waiting for me, and she had a new case for me. After my Father and Mother had gone to work, she took me to our neighbor's door. This was Mr. and Mrs. Brown's home. He was the one in need off my help. He was an agoraphobic, and he hadn't left his house in years. And was a considerable problem because his business was raising exotic hens, that produced the most desirable eggs Birmingham had ever seen. So, how was he to present his eggs if he couldn't go outside? The customers couldn't all fit in his small house. Therefore his wife wanted me to cure him of his agoraphobia.

Mr. Shelby Brown was truly creative in creating his quality product. In spite of the coal dust soil in his backyard, he had managed to grow grass, so his hens were grass fed. But, even though they went into their cages at night, a cat could get at them.

An even greater problem was the loss of money from t the egg cases along the sidewalk. Too often, money and eggs were stolen. And my buddy, Shorty, was one of the stealers, but fortunately, his father made him return the stolen goods. So, it seems that checks were working on his kleptomaniac.

But, Auntie Jessica always brought her money up to the Brown's front door. And that's where she brought me the first day I was back home. Mrs. Ellie Brown met us there, and eagerly led me to her husband, who was also eager to met me.

"I've heard all about you, son, from Auntie Jessie, and I hope you can help me. As you know, because of my problem, I'm losing money.

"And as I'm sure my practical Auntie Jessie, told you I don't cost anything.""

"Well, that's also important, but more important, she assures me you can fix me."

"Sir, not only am I confident that I can fix you, because you are such a good and community worthwhile person, I am eager to fix you. So, here's what we're going to do. Let's clear room on this carpeted floor. Now, stand up straight with your back toward me. Now, I want you to trust me. We are going to do what's called a trust fall, which mean you have to trust me to catch you before your head hits this heavy glass jar I am going to place where your head might hit the floor. So, are you going to trust me?"

He hesitated briefly, then said, "Yes."

Fortunately, since Mr. Brown was not too much taller than my now ten year old body, I would have no trouble catching him. So, I said, "Let's do it!"

And we did, but as he was falling, I kicked the jar out of the way and kicked a soft pillow where his head would hit the floor. But, I did this quietly so he couldn't hear what I did. But he could definitely feel that I was moving out from behind him and was not going to catch him.

He screamed, and tried to stop himself with his arms, but it was too late. But, as I had planned his head hit the soft pillow.

When he realized he wasn't hurt, he stopped screaming. Then asked, "But why did you trick me like that? I thought you wanted me to trust you?"

"Trust is a part of whatever I do when I am attempting to aid people. And it is a part of my way of fixing you. SSo, let me explain. What you felt at that last moment, when you feared you were going to bash you head, was panic. Now, panic is both good and bad. If a wolf is chasing you, panic will give you the strength to climb up a tall tree so the the wolf can't reach you. But if there is no wolf chasing you, your panic is a waste of energy, and if you are too often in panic, you will likely get sick, have trouble sleeping, lose weight, and, as in your case, develop agoraphobia so you won't feel that terrible panic. Make sense?"

Without hesitation, my new, and now more eager than evert, shouted, "Yes!" But then, after hesitation, he asked, "But is indoors, but what about outdoors.?"

"Good question, my young patient" I laughed. Now comes the outdoors. But first, lie here on the floor, and breathe deeply. Deep breathing is the best tool against anxiety. Good, again, and again, and again. Now get up, tale my hand, close your eyes, and let's walk to through the door that goes outside. No! Don't open your eyes, just stand still and imagine what's out there. See your egg boxes. See the green trees across the street. Now see the blue sky and balmy clouds beyond the trees. And now take another deep breath . . . and slowly open your eyes."

"God, how I've missed this! What have I done to myself?"

"Only given m in being human. And humans make mistakes, and being human you made a mistake. Now let's go back inside, rest a moment, and we'll let your long enduring wife continue the fixing you process."

"Amen!" cried Mrs. Brown.

"And one more thing before I turn you over yourself your wife, there will no doubt be times when the Panic Devil will show up to haunt you. When he does, just shout, Get behind me, Devil! I'm in charge of me now!"

Then I ended with, "Then the new Mr. Brown will take charge and repeat what we just did, and maybe again and again."

STRESS MANAGEMENT

Enduring Pain is usually Insane

Many athletic trainers say,
"No pains, no gains!"
But I say these athletic trainers
Have muscles that they are using as brains.
They don't seem to realize
That the only thing that pain is good for
Is to tell you what not to do,
And if you continue in pain,
Your life could be prematurely through.
So, only endure a lot of pain
Only if there is some or a lot of life to gain.
Otherwise, you painfilled life
Will go down the drain.

I was twelvears old when my grammer school recreation teacher, Mrs. Lovenin, called me into her office. "Danny," she said, "This our high school coach, Sandy Getter." "Please to meet you I said," respectfully. "And this is someone I know you must have heard of, Amy Fasiter, the wonder women who is going to be our next Olypicpic quarter miler."

I was immediately interested. My track distance was also the quarter mile, and I was training for the city wide city track meet. But then I looked more closely at Ammy, and all I saw was a beautiful young girl who I was falling in love with.

"And Danny, she needs your special kind of help. How about it."

"Any thing I whispered to myself. But then I looked more closely at Amy. As I first saw her with my love blind eyes, she was absolutely beautiful, but now when I considered helping her, I could see she was not the perfect beautiful athlete she was supposed to be. Her complextion was sallow, not rosy, almost gray. And she looked weak, not stong and ready to run. What had happed to her?

Her coach explained. "All the college coaches who want to be her Olympic coach, are telling her that she has to train harder if she wants to be ready for the Olypmpics and she tries to please them. But now we and even she are begining to realize that they are not helping her, the are only wearing her down!"

Then, for the first time, Ammy spoke up, almost with tears in her eyes, "Yes, Danny, please, please help me!"

Without hesitating, I said, "I will, and we will begin right now! So, Amy, you have your track shoes with you, and your shorts. I need to be driven by my house, it's on the way to Leagend Field where we will begin our treatment. Mrs. Lovenin, please tell the principle I'll be missing class."

"He won't be worrried, Danny. You're way ahead in your classes."

We had no trouble getting into Legion Field. The guard recognize Amy, and I guess he'd be watching this potential Olympic champion from the stands, so he could tell his kids.

Amy and I went into our starting stantes, and before I say "Start!" she had alreadu dashed off.

"Stop!" I shouted. "Listen, young lady, "I tell you when to start, not your overtrained brain. So, get back here, listen to what your new, much wiser coach is telling you."

A subdued, and maybe even somewhat cowed super aththelet, said, "Yes sir."

I

.But enough of my coddling you. Let me get serious and tell you how and why I will be coaching you in a certain way. Your body has been abused. It needs to repair itself. In our every run, you will never go at top speed. That's just for an actual event. Understand?"

"I understand Coach!"

"And from point on, you must do this everyday: eat three meals a day, consisting of berries, nuts, greens, and egg and eggs, drink lots of water, and breathe deeply before exercising.

And that was the routine for the next weeks, which I believed was long enough for Amy's damaged body to recoveer. Although, the other coaches from the other high school teams knew Ammy's coach Getter, but this 12 year so called coach was an anomily, but Amy's stare said, "He's my coach, so back off!"

They did. Then I instructed Amy to soften up her compition before each meet and wish hem well, and assure them that she would also be doing her best against such stiff comption

And then I reminded Amy, as she begain each race, in her starting position, take and hold a deep breath. Then go.

And finally, I reminded Amy start off slowly. Let another runner set the pase. Only at toware the end should she dash ahead. After all, these girls were nowhere near as fast as she, so she didn't need to undermine her body's recovery in this not too important race.

Of course, she did as she was told, and she looked only moderately pleased with herself. That pleasure would be hers at the State Track Championship.

With that thought, I told Ammy that I believed my coaching job was done. I believed that she had done everything I had asked of her, and I believed that she meant what she said when she reassured me that she felt stong now and would continue to feel strong because she would do exactly what I had taught her. But, I expected her to be thinking of me as she received Olympic Gold Metal.

She kissed me, as assured me she would.

ANGER MANAGEMENT

Happy makes the Heart grow Fonder

Always being angry isn't good for your heart.
Your blood pressure's up, your pulse is racing,
And your life could be over
Before it's off to a good start.

So, take a deep breath, and let it out,
And then another deep breath,
And then hold it in before you're able
To let out an angry shout.

And just as important,
The person you shouted at won't get so angry at you
That he has to make sure
That your angry life is through.

Efvien Walker was a park ranger, and also an avid envirnmentalist. His ten year old son, Efven Junior was one of my classmates. He stop me after school, obviously upset. "I really need your help, Danny, my father . . . my father almost hit me."

I took it from Junior's shocked expression that this was not what his father would do. "I'm guessing that he's never hit you, but what made him so angry this time?"

"Oh, he's always angry, he just holds it back."

"Always?"

"When he's hiking on the Park trails, and he sees someone tossing trash about, he says he has to grit his teeth and restrain himself, because he wants to knock the trasher's head off."

"So, what does he do with his anger?'

"Nothing. He tells me he doesn't know what to do. It take all his energy just to control his anger. So, can you help us.?"

"I'll do my best. I've noticed that he picks you up after school. I believe that's him now. Do you think he will accept my help?"

"I'm sure he will. I've already told him about you, and he didn't even hesitate in saying yes. That's how desperate he is."

Junior was obviously right. When I introduced myself, this six foot two, very muscular man, hopped out of his Jeep and vigorously shook my hand. "Thank you so much, Daniel, I'll do anything you asked. Almost hitting my son is something I never want to happen again!"

I withdrew my crushed hand and shook it,. Then I laughed, "I'm glad you didn't hit me instead."

As we drove to the park, since Ranger Walker was so eager, I started **my** treatment **right** away. "Ranger Walker, am I right in assuming that the environment is a passion for you, so anything that violate that passion deserves punishment?"

He shook his head, yes.

But I also believe that you are a gentle person, and do not believe you have the right to hurt other people Right?"

"Right."

"So, you're really caught in a dilemma. How does that affect your health?"

"I can't sleep at night, I get indigestion, and just generally feel rotten."

My plan, which must become your plan, has many parts. You need to strengthen you body. So, I want you to eat three small meals a day, consisting of berries, nuts, leafy vegetables, and some protein, like eggs, fish, and dairy products."

"I can do that."

"I can do it too!" volunteered Junior."

"And, since you probably squirm about in bed, I would guess you sleep alone so as to not disturb your wife. So, starting to tonight, I want you to make your bedroom as dark as possible, shut out all noise, and sleep on your side, in the nude. That's so any nigh-clothes don't bunch up about you and disturb your sleep."

We had just reach the family house, so I said, "Let's start another part of out plan."

We went to his bedroom, where I had him lie down on his back, and start his breathing training.

"Now, I want to take a four deep breaths. Then fifteen quick shallow breathes, and then, while thinking of nothing take fifteen more breaths. Now, Elven, you're feeling very relaxed you are are almost felling asleep, but not quite. You feel more like you're dreaming, but yet controling your dream. Now, in your almost-dream, fell yourself walking along the Park trail with Junior. Up ahead, you see many trail walkers, and sure enough, they are tossing trash alongside the trail. So, you draw in several deep breaths, and politely say, "Sir, I'm sure you're enjoying these beautiful woods so much, you're just not thinking what you're doing. So, sir, please gather your trash, and any other trash you see. And place it in the trash basket up head. And thank you, sir, for protecting our Park."

"Okay, Elven, take several short breaths, and lie still while I describe tomorrow's plan. It's a weekend, so there will be many people walking in the Park. And, of course, they will be trashing. But, just like you did in you your dream state, you will cleverly shame them into doing what you want them to do. Okay?"

"Okay."

"Good. Now wake up your son. He's still in his dream Park."

Junior. shot up, "I'm not, I'm awake!" and he almost fell down trying to get up too quickly.

The next day, Saturday, and, as in his dream, the thoughtless trashers were doing their thing. And just as in his dream, Elven took deep breaths, and politely asked the trashers to do what they now realized they should do. And soon, the trash baskets were full.

Then, a relieved Elven smiled at me and said, "Daniel, you are not a young Psychologist, you are a woodland elf, and you cast a spell on me and cured me of my anger. I'll never be angry again!"

And so to test him, this evil wood elf tossed some trash onto the side of the trail, and laughed evilly.

Then he smiled benignly, softly saying, "Would you please pick up that trash . . . or else I'll knock your head off!"

PSYCHOSES

Or Nuts?

Some people say you are crazy.
You think people are after you,
You see things that aren't there,
You don't move, even though you can.
So you belong in an asylum,
To keep you out of normal people's hair.

But I say you're just different,
And your difference could be good.
And you just need to use your difference
To do all the good things that you should.

So, carry on Crazy Person,
And let those normal people stand aside.
And while you're out doing different good things,
Let those normal people go to an asylum to hide.

I was now twelve years old, and my Granny and Granddaddy Broxton wanted to see me before I began thinking of myself as to big too hang around with my grandparents. So, I decided to spend the night with them. They lived about a mile from my house, so, just like when I was six years old, I walked there in the late afternoon.

They live at 906 and 1/2 Cotton Avenue. The 1/2 meant second floor, and I remember, sitting in my Grandfather's lap listening to what he called locusts, singing up in the tall oak trees. They were no doubt the kadidids that come out every seven years or so. But whatever they were, the constant chattering almost put me to sleep.

But Granddad's twelve year old grandson, Sunday morning, walked two blocks to the Methdist Church to hear Reverend Lester give a rather solum sermon about what was happening in Europe, and whether it was our Christian reponsibility to aid our allies, the British, or was it our Christians duty to avoid war.

The church addandants and I were as solumn as was the Reverend, and I realized that as a young Amercan, I should learn more about what was happening overseas.

But, when my grandparents and I was leaving the Church, and the Reverend asked to see me in his office, I realized something more personal for the Reverend was going on.

Then he asked my grandparents if he might speak to me alone. They looked uncertain, but I assured them when I understod what was going on, I would would come back to their apparment to explain why the Reverand wanted to speak to me alone.

As Reverand Lester took me his house nextdoor, he told me about his son, Ezikial, who had been in his first year in college, and had been planning to be a mimister like his father, but had stopped studying, left college, and came back here to me."

When we entered Ezikial's room, I saw exactly what I expected. Ezikial was a handsom young man who resembled his father, although he was an inch or so taller. This was a young man who would have made a fine minister. But this was a sad and nervous young man who might be doomed to be a chronic psychotic if I couldn't come up with some plan to help him.

Reverend Lister explained immediately. "My son, Ezekial, has been dianosed as psychotic, and his psychitrist has perscribed anti-psychotic medications, but my son won't stay on them, even though they reduce his hallucinationss. He says they make him too drowsy.

"I've heard that happens," I said."

"I know you must have," he continued, "My colored janitor told how you helped your neighbor manage is phobias, even without medication. So, I'm asking, no begging, you to help him.

"No need to beg, Reverend, a caring father diserves my help. Please, may I meet your son?"

"Thank you, yes, he's in his room upstairs"

"Okay, Doctor Daneil, do your thing!" I said to myself.

Ezikial was sitting at his desk staring at an unoped book. I slid a chair beside his desk, and addressed him firmly, "Ezikial, look at me!"

He jerked his chair around and stared at me briefly before speaking. "Dad, who is this boy? I don't need a boy to help me."

I answered before his father. "I'm not just a boy, I'm the knowledgeable and dedicated person who is going to train you to manage you psychosis, and I'm going to do this without demanding that you always stay on your medication."

The anoyed expression on his face suddenly turned to hope. "You can do that?" he asked.

"No, *we* can do that. This is going to be *our* project, which you can abandon any time you wish. What do you say, shall we do it?"

Without hesidation, he answered, "Yes."

Then I heard a great sigh coming from his father.

"Good, but first some science. Your brain is an amazing instutrament. You don't have to be carzy to see and hear things that aren't there. You do that all the time while draming. Your problem is, you do those those while awake. Well, what I want us to do is give you control of you brain so you can see and hear things only when you want to. Or, even when you can't, to not be bother by your lack of control. But, of course, you have to get enough control that you don't do anything foolish when you're not in control. But, that's when you will, temprarily need your meds."

"Temporary, you're sure?"

"It's up to you."

"Now lie down on your bed and close your eyes. Then take several deep breathes, and then totally relax. Now, maintaining control of your mind like I said you could, you're going to take an imaginary trip. You're stroling along along a trail through the woods, and there is a small stream moving along beside the trail. And now you see small fish jumping up and back into the stream. Then, overhead, you hear birds in the trees singing, and the rhythem of their peeping seems to match the slow movement of your steeps.

"Now, Ezekiel, swithch you attention from what you see and hear to what you feel. Are you still relaxed?

"Yes."

"Do you still feel in control of your mind, of your thoughts and feelings?

"Yes, yes I do!"

"So does this mean you're not crazy?"

This time he did hesitate. "I . . . I don't know."

"Good again. The right answer. Control of your so called psychotic mind is a skill that requires practice, mabe a lifetime of practice, but I believe you are off to a good start."

"So do I!" said Reverend L, "Praise God All Mighty, so do I!

Then Ezekial changed that, "No, praise Doctor Daniel!"

The next morning, we left Reverned Lester behind, and Ezikiel drove us to park outside a cemutary on the right side of the road leading South out of town. Across the street was what was known as Indian Mountain. It was said to be a burial mound for a long vanished Native American Nation. I had climbed the trail to the top several times as a child. I felt it was sacret to me.

Ezikiel had never climbed it, so as I explained it history, I described how we would use it to help him manage is problem. "Yesterday, you mastered your brain troubles by using fantasy. Today, you will master your troubled brain in reality. So, let's start up the trail. You go ahead of me. Now, tell me what you feel as you observe what is happening around you."

Ezikiel did this with no trouble, and when we reached the top of the small mountain, he let out a long sigh, and merely said, "That was easy, so I guess that means you finished your work, and now my continued improvement is up to me."

"If that's what you want, then that's alright with me."

"It is what I want, so now what are you going to do"?

"I'll get to that in a moment, but first one last question for you. Now that you're mastering your mind, what are you going to do with your time?"

"That's easy, finish what I started, and what Dad wants me to to, go back to the University, finish my Religious Degree and become an effective, though somewhat weird Methodist Misister . . . and maybe specialize in serving crazy people like I was. How's that for irony? Now what about you?"

"I know. How about I write long book called, *A Very Psychologist is Born,* sell it, make a lot of money, and retire young."

"Right! And we both laughed at that.

OTHER BOOKS BY THE AUTHOR

D. B. Clark is the author of: *The Way to Levi, 1ˢᵗ Edition* (Kendall Hunt Publishing Co), *To Lead the Way, The End of Ohm, The Way Beyond, Self-Development and Transcendence, Ashes to Ashes, A Heaven of Hell, Thoughts Along the Way, The Way Beyond, Mother Rat & Love is Eternal, Left of the Right World, Beyond Forever, On the Shoulder of Giants* (all universe, Inc. *Forever Young, It could be Verse, Love and Roses, Mercury Smiled, Death: a Second Opinion, Poems from a Smorgasbord Mind, War: A Love-Hate, Relationship, Didactics, Affirmation, My Modern Haiku, Archives Volume One, The Way to L'vei, The Curse of Humorous Verse, These Poems be Philosophy, This Garden Earth, Chronicle One through Chronicle Thirty-Seven Honoring My Beloved Brother, Modern Metaphysical Verse, Paradise Reconsidered, My Best to You, Once Upon a Time, Wisdom in Verse, Sagacious or Silly Sayings, A Modern Mother Goose, More Medical Mirth, Even More Medical Mirth, Arguing With God, If I Learn, So Can You, A Poetic Fix for Politics, How it Really Happened, Terse Verse is Better Not Worse, Let Us War No More, These are My Best, Modern Aesop fables, Laughing at Myself, Poemmettes, Children Do Play with Dead Things, The New Devil's Dictionary, These are My Latest Best # Three, Four and Five, Once Upon a Time Again, Beyond Forever, Poemettes Three, Who an I, and Why?),* The Autobiography of D. B. Clark, Sagacious or Silly Sayings # 2 Expanded, Once Upon a Time Three, *These are My Latest Best # Six, My Latest Best # Seven,* ((All by Lulu.com)*Poems will Make you Wiser, Aging, an Option, Dr Clark's Health Management Plan (These are My Latest Best # Six* all, lulu.

com),The Autobiography of D. B. Clark, Sagacious or Silly Sayings # 2 Expanded, Once Upon a Time Three, *These are My Latest Best # 2, 3, 4, 5, 6, 7,*(All by Lulu.com)and *Growing Beyond the Fathers* (PublishAmerica, Inc*).*

If you have enjoyed reading this book, you might also like reading these books by D. B. Clark.

Forever Young, This Garden Earth, There are My Best Poems of 2019, The Ever Returning Life of Robison Buddy Sreets (Lulu.com) Poems Promoting Painless Dying (Iuniverse.com) My Three Favorite Novels (Iuniverse.com) (Iuniverse.com)

THE AUTHOR'S BIO

D B. Clark is a retired Clinical Psychologist and college professor who has publish textbooks, novels, and around 90 books of poetry. with 40 years of assisting clients become more effective in living. His attempt to manage his own health is documented in his book, Dr Clark's Health Maintenance Plan.

Also, tread D.B.Clark's dally poems on <u>*donald71@allpotry.com*</u> *where people from all over the would read and praise his poems.*